FOUNDATIONS

A Primer for Healthy Church Membership

Victor R. Scott

The Foundry Press

Columbus, Georgia

ISBN-13: 978-1-942221-05-0 (paperback)
ISBN-13: 978-1-942221-06-7 (MOBI)
ISBN-13: 978-1-942221-07-4 (EPUB)

The
Foundry
Press

An imprint of Scott Publishing Services
Columbus, Georgia

scottpublishingservices@gmail.com

To

Pastor David Thompson

Because he spoke the truth in love.

"Have I then become your enemy by telling
you the truth?" Gal. 4:16, ESV

.

TABLE OF CONTENTS

INTRODUCTION

We All Have Growing Pains

I vividly remember waking up as a young boy in the middle of the night, pain shooting up both of my shins. My immediate thought was that someone had come into my room after I had fallen asleep and hit me as hard as they could. This may have been the overactive imagination of a child, but I will never forget what I felt. The sensation was like someone had put a vice across both of my shins and had begun tightening and then loosening the vice over and over again. I had never felt pain like that in my life. Now, I was about twelve years old, so at the time I did not have a lot of other moments to compare it too.

The next morning, I told my mom what happened and she told me it was a normal part of getting bigger. They were just "growing pains." That was not all that comforting. I knew that I would be doing more growing and the prospect of experiencing more of those painful events was not something I was looking forward to.

It has been a long time since I had physical growing pains like I did that night, but the experience of growing pains has not disappeared and, in many respects, has not changed as I have gotten older. The growing pains have just shifted from the physical aspects of life to the spiritual and emotional ones. The process of maturing is one of the realities of life that cannot be avoided. No one is immune from the realities of growing up. For some people growing up is something to look forward to (wanting to turn sixteen and finally get that driver's license). For others growing up is something to avoid (having to pay the bills on your own!).

One of the more valuable lessons from my late night experience was that I learned that I am constantly learning new things about myself and even others. Some of these lessons are easier to deal with and accept. Others, I wish I never had to go through. Regardless of the reason or the effect I would not change any of them today. Each of these events has shaped who I am.

Growing pains are not necessarily meant to be

enjoyed (although they may not all be negative or painful), but they are a necessary facet of life. Growing pains serve as a sign that we are alive and that we are not perfect. Both of these are good things. The challenge is to remain an active participant in the process. I had to accept the pains as a reality I could learn from because there will never be just one. I will experience growing pains for as long as I live. Even when I may have a desire to lean towards quitting or giving up rather than fighting through the pain, I have to remember that I will get through it. I have to fight against this tendency to surrender to the challenges of life.

As I was growing up, my father had a unique style for disciplining the children. The majority of the time there was no corporal punishment if we could answer one question. The question was my father's way of gaging if we were growing in wisdom, even at a young age. The question was, "Did you learn anything?" If we could provide an answer then our punishment was greatly reduced. However, if we could not he would provide an answer and then meet out appropriate discipline. It was never a good idea not to have an answer. We knew what was coming and we were required to give an answer, so we knew it was best to be ready.

This principle of discipline has served me well as I became an adult. Many of my other life experiences have also helped to form how I deal with growing pains. With each event I ask myself the question my father taught me and I seek to understand what there is to learn. The effort and practice of self-reflection is an important skill we all must learn. The longer we wait to think upon what we have experienced the harder it is to remember any potential lessons our growing pains may offer to us.

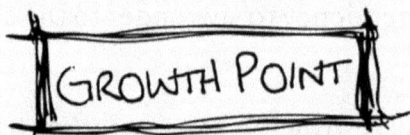

GROWTH POINT

Think back to a time where you experienced a growing pain. What was it? What did you learn from it?

How did that event affect future behavior?

Growing Edges

My pastor told me, as I sat across from him in his office during one of my annual staff reviews, "We all have growing edges." I was not exactly sure what he meant. And, to be honest, I was not sure I wanted to know. He went on to explain that a growing edge is a place in our lives and character where we have room to improve, get better. We all have them. (Denying it is proof that we do!) We all have several of them. We may not always see them or even be willing to accept them, but they are there. Their presence is why we need someone to remind us of where we need to grow; of where we have room to improve. The same is true in the church.

As members of a local church we have to grow together, together. What this means is that all the members of the church should participate in fostering a healthy church environment. The pastor cannot keep a church healthy by shear will power. To have this expectation of the lead pastor is unfair and unrealistic. While the pastor(s) may have a particular responsibility within the church, they do not possess everything within themselves to maintain the health of the church.

This one misconception (among a few others) is what makes a church's growing pains difficult and different from our individual growing pains. They are difficult because they involve more than one person addressing and working through their own personal growing edges. Because we are all growing and changing when the focus changes to the church it can become easy to minimize our own issues and fixate on the issues we see in the church.

We have to understand that we are all involved in the process of helping one another become who Jesus died for us to become. The difficulty we face is that all of the people in our church may not always be on the same page. We may be in different stages of life, different levels of maturity (both personal and spiritual), and having experienced different events that shaped our thoughts and character qualities. All of these aspects of life, and more, play a role in how we interact with others and especially other members of our local church body.

GROWTH POINT

Identify three areas of your life that could be considered growing edges. (*If you cannot think of any ask a friend you trust.*)

1.

2.

3.

The Purpose of this Book

This book is designed so it can be used by an individual or as a group study. In both cases, the reader will be challenged to look at seven of the most common aspects of the Christian life. It is my conviction that these seemingly ordinary facets of the Christian life are not so ordinary after all. They actually represent the key strategic behaviors and priorities every believer should contemplate as they grow in their commitment to Jesus. Because of this, I call them FOUNDATIONS. They serve as the building blocks for a healthy Christian life and a healthy church.

As we proceed, it will be beneficial to think about and establish a clear statement regarding the church's purpose. So, for the purpose of this book we will define the church in the following way.

The church has been designed by God to reproduce the life of Christ in each of her members.

The significance of this statement is it provides a clear means of thinking and talking about the church. This definition will also help us to diagnose whatever issues may need to be addressed. My hope is that when we achieve greater spiritual health as individual believers the whole of the church is blessed.

A secondary assumption that will help guide our discussion throughout this book is that the Bible's basic premise is that to be a Christian is to be a member of the church. Chapter 4 discusses the concept in more detail but, it is still worth stating here. Hopefully, during the course of this study the reader will be able to see the need to address and manage these growing edges in their life in light of these two inseparable realities.

Over the next few pages we will look at seven areas that every Christian should know, understand and practice. Each of these are both growing pains for a believer and growing edges for the church. Each of these areas are important because they are the visible realities of our faith. Keep in mind that considering and modifying these areas of your life does not win you "brownie points" with God. The idea here is to become more aware of our need for mature and responsible thinking as it concerns our spiritual growth and our relationship to our family of faith, the church.

Also, these outward manifestations of our faith can serve as the readily identifiable demonstrations of our personal growth and understanding. When we see change occurring in these areas we can know that God is at work. This is both a blessing and a reminder to continue growing. There is no end to our journey of becoming more Christ-like. Our ultimate goal should drive us to be constantly growing and learning how to be more like our Savior, Jesus.

At any given time any person that is not a Christian, not a part of the body of Christ, will come in contact with a believer who may be (should be?) engaging in these activities. It is at these times that we discover where we are and whether or not we are moving towards where we need to be. We are called to be a light to the world. If this is to be true for us, then we must strive for greater obedience and submission to the sanctifying work of the Holy Spirit in the areas we will discuss below.

The journey of becoming fully engaged members of the church requires us to do some deep searching within our own heart and minds. Do we want healthier churches? Could our relationships with our brothers and sisters in Christ be stronger? Healthier? Transformation can be exciting and simple, but it was never intended to be easy. Just ask the caterpillar.

My mom's explanation helped me to understand what my body was going through. My pastor's reminder gave me hope for my own growth and development. My desire is that over the next few chapters we will see the purpose of these pains and find a way to endure them and grow because of them. With God's grace we may get to the point where we can see the benefits of what is happening, even when we do not always understand or enjoy it. As we begin this journey, take a risk, discover something new, and choose to grow by seeing the purpose in the process.

FOUNDATION 1

Fellowship

What If I Don't Know Them?

There are so many things about a church that can be uncomfortable for new people. Even if you have been going to church for a long time, moving to a new city and finding a new church can be difficult. There are probably many reasons to feel uncomfortable, but one of the primary sources of discomfort is simply meeting new people. As members of the church it is part of our job to make guests feel like family. This does not mean that they will immediately be invited to our homes for dinner. What it does mean is that we will do our best to show hospitality to those who are searching for a place to belong.

The first foundation we are looking at is

FELLOWSHIP. As church members we have to understand what we are talking about when we talk about fellowship. Fellowship is more than just being in the same room as someone else or even saying "hello" to those around us. Fellowship is found, not in the buildings where we meet nor in the restaurants that have great atmosphere. True and lasting fellowship is about the relationships we establish and foster with other Christians, particularly within our local congregation.

Fellowship is the sharing of our lives. It is coming to a place where those who at one time were strangers to us have now become family. Those people who before we would have seen only once in a while, now, for some reason, we find ourselves thinking about and wanting to be around them more and more. Fellowship is the process where another person's life becomes a part of our own life. Their story becomes a part of our story. This is the goal of true Christian fellowship. It is genuine and sincere.

One common misconception about fellowship is that we will be able to share the same level of fellowship with every member of our church. This is both unrealistic and impractical. We will have greater intimacy and relationship with some members of our congregations. However, the idea of fellowship we are discussing here has to do with the way our hearts respond and feel toward those who are a part of our church. Healthy fellowship, in the end, has to do with how we receive those who are a part of the Christian community.

A second misconception about fellowship is that we may become intrusive in other Christian's lives. Fellowship is an invitation. We are inviting another person into the full range of our lives. It does not happen all at once. We are looking to build the kind of relationship that both honors God and edifies us. It may be hard to believe, but in the process these new people, these strangers, may even become intimate members of our inner circle. When another person becomes a "loved one," so that you hurt because they hurt, that is fellowship. This is not an easy road to travel, the one called fellowship. It is a slow and sometimes hurtful journey to bring people in close. It is not easy, but there is something about being able to share our lives with someone, about having another to journey down life's road.

Will we be able to have fellowship with everyone in the church in the same way? As I mentioned before that is not possible, and I do not think this should be the goal. The question we should ask ourselves is this, what are we doing to reach out and make a difference in other people's lives? Are we willing to consider our own prejudices and hang-ups to reach out to those around us? Do we have the courage to do something that makes us uncomfortable and invite someone into our lives?

Fellowship can be difficult. But, it does not need to be made impossible. If we work to make fellowship a reality in our churches, we will see transformation in the lives of those around us, and hopefully in ourselves as well.

GROWTH POINT

What obstacles do you see in building stronger relationships with those around you in your church?

Name three ways you can become more intentional in fostering true fellowship among your brothers and sisters in Christ.

1.

2.

3.

Why Is Fellowship Important?

Lasting spiritual growth is maximized in an environment where trust exists. If we do not trust those around us, how will we feel safe enough to grow? One of the most difficult aspects of growing in faith is being able to share our genuine concerns and struggles while at the same time knowing that these issues will not become the talk of the town, or worse, the church. We cannot worship in an environment where we feel we are being isolated or shunned. Healthy Christian fellowship provides the foundation for building safe environments for those who desire to grow in their faith.

In the simplest of terms, trust is built by being trustworthy. Similarly, love is known by being loving. Fellowship comes to life and is experienced when we are neighbors to strangers and family to friends. It is the movement from not knowing to being known.

This may seem like a difficult way of doing it, but that is what Jesus did for us. The apostle Paul writes it this way, "While we were still sinners, Christ died for us" (Rom 5:8; NKJV). Jesus took the risk to come into the world and become something he was not. He was not a man and yet he became incarnate. He knew nothing of sin, and yet he became sin so that we could experience his righteousness. Jesus is the ultimate example of what it means to fellowship with those around you. He did not judge anyone, but loved all he came in contact with. Did everyone appreciate him for it? No. Did that stop him from being loving to those around him? No, it did not.

A large part of what makes fellowship what it ought to be comes from the way we react to the people and circumstances around us, we should ask ourselves, "Do we even want fellowship to exist?" Then we must be the first to exhibit the fruit of the Spirit among the saints (Gal 5:22-23). These are the tools we are given to create an environment that will produce spiritual fellowship. To answer the question a little more directly—"Why is fellowship important?—we need to understand that it is within the context of fellowship that we love one another as Jesus instructs and that people will become convinced that we are Christ's disciples (Jn 13:35).

Jesus told us that our communion with one another in the fellowship we share is one of the key indicators of his presence within us. I wonder if we have ever considered the impact our lack of fellowship has on those who are not a part of the church. Could it be that one of the main reasons the world outside the church does not care to be a part of the world inside the church is due to our inconsistencies in how we fellowship?

GROWTH POINT

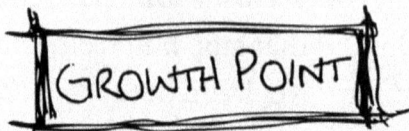

Have there been any ways in which you have undervalued the fellowship in your church?

Why do you think fellowship is not seen as an important part of the Christian experience?

How Do We Sustain Fellowship?

Here is where the rubber meets the road, so to speak. How do we make a genuine effort to sustain fellowship within a church? The word that comes to mind is **sincerity**. The word sincere comes from a very old word that means pure or unmixed. Fundamentally we are talking about a pure and truthful quality regarding what we are talking about. When we demonstrate sincerity we are being our truest selves. When we apply this idea to the body of Christ, we are embodying all the best characteristics of Jesus within and throughout the life of the church.

If true and lasting fellowship is going to exist there has to be sincerity between those who are living and working within the body of Jesus. If what we do is half-hearted or selfish, fellowship will not grow and it will eventually die. The challenge for every church is to act quickly if these attitudes enter into the body. More to the point, if we are not committed to the priority of fellowship among the members of the church, this lack of conviction to promote healthy fellowship will quickly be found out by those around us, both inside and outside our local congregation.

Fellowship will happen when we decide that we are really going to care about those that come to our church, whether visitor or member, we will love them with the love of God. The beauty of fellowship is the unity that it creates. This unity is the distinguishing element of the Christian church. Jesus understood that our move out of from under the influence of the world requires a new community, a community he provided for us, his followers in the church.

GROWTH POINT

What are some reason we find it difficult to be sincere?

FOUNDATION 2

Ministry

In the next two chapters we will look at two sides of the same coin, ministry and service. In this chapter we will first look at ministry. When we talk about ministry we will be looking at what the members do together when the church is working as a corporate body. In other words, we will be considering how we, as members of Christ's body, are to be working together to accomplish the purposes and mission of Jesus through the church, which is his body on Earth. In the next chapter we will look at service as the individual outworking of our faith in our individual lives and how this works together with the church's mission.

Am I a Minister?

I have heard many believers ask this question in different forms and I would like to say that the answer to this question is yes–and no. It is a definite "yes" because if we have accepted the salvation Jesus Christ died to provide, a bond has been made. Jesus' desires should now become our desires. By virtue of this relationship with and in Christ we are called to participate in Jesus' ministry in the world. We all are to be equipped for ministry by the leaders of the church and are encouraged to share and speak about the faith that we now profess to live. Our lives are no longer our own. Because we no longer belong to ourselves it is vital that we recognize that there is a corporate reality we should grapple with and embrace.

Peter speaks about the *priesthood* of *all believers,* which implies that there is a shared responsibility among all believers to minister to the world (1 Pet 2:4-10). This ministry is not explicitly describing public preaching or evangelistic endeavors, even though some of this may be included. As followers of Jesus we cannot dismiss the ministry component of our faith journey because we are uncomfortable, afraid, or insecure. Ministry should be seen as a necessary reality in all of our lives. The challenge we face is discovering the role we are going to play in the greater ministry of the church and then fulfilling it.

But, the answer to the question "Am I a minister?" is also "no." It is "no" because not all who believe in Jesus are called to be pastors, teachers or evangelists. Not everyone is called to preach and to stand in front of the entire church and exhort a congregation. Not everyone is called to be a preacher because there must be a particular desire, an unquenchable passion for the word and work of Jesus Christ, and a willingness to share in leading the church in this way. Ultimately, the particular calling of a few does not negate the general call to all demonstrated by our willingness to be a part of the work God has for us to participate in. We all are called to be in ministry.

Part of the problem may be that the image of ministry has been distorted in the church to mean full-time, vocational ministry. This however, is not what the Bible teaches on the subject. Not being a full-time minister does not relieve any of us from our responsibility to model, tell, and live out our faith every day. We must learn and expect for the life and death of Christ to influence every facet of our lives as we live before the world. Every single believer in Jesus Christ must be engaged in the spreading of the Gospel. That is the undeniable truth of the Great Commission (Mt 28:19-20). No one is exempt from being an intentional witness to the Gospel's power and truth.

GROWTH POINT

Have you ever considered ministry as something you should do because you are a Christian? Why or why not?

How do you feel about the prospect of seeking opportunities of ministering to those around you?

Ministry Is Not an Option

After Jesus' crucifixion and resurrection, Jesus wanted to confirm that Peter had been restored even though Peter had denied Jesus. It is interesting that Jesus gave Peter the same number of opportunities to accept Jesus' assignment for his life (Jn 21:15-19). Having done so, Jesus sent Peter to feed His lambs. While the command to feed Jesus' lambs is found within a specific personal and historical context, I believe that it contains a much more general command, one that applies to us today. This command is one we must listen to if we claim to love Jesus. To follow Jesus is to walk where He walked, doing what He did, with love and grace.

When we identify with Jesus we are buying into the ministry He came to bring. Don't underestimate the implication of this. Our relationship with Jesus is an "all-in" proposition. The Great Commission reveals this to us. Jesus, once He had suffered, was crucified, died, and was resurrected, did not leave this earth without leaving some final instructions. He knew there would be some confusion without him present. There was work left to be done and that work was going to fall on the shoulders of those he left behind. These disciples would have the responsibility of continuing what Jesus started. Let's consider a question: Do you know when the church will no longer have to worry about spreading the Gospel? *When we all are in heaven.* This may sound overly dramatic, but it is not. It is the undeniable responsibility left to Jesus first disciples and every generation of disciples ever since Jesus ascended back to heaven.

Ministry is **not** an option for the Christ follower. Some may feel that they are exempt because they do not know enough or because they have not been Christians long enough. These are not valid reasons for not ministering to those around us. The most basic Christian responsibility is to love one another. This is the beginning of our ministry as a member of the church, the body of Christ.

It is possible that the reason we fail to be in ministry is because we do not recognize that ministry, at its center, is about having a heart of service (we will cover this more in depth in the next chapter). We are called to serve one another. This is one of the most vivid images Jesus left us. He told his disciples that the greatest in the kingdom would be the servant of all (Mk 9:35). What's more, Jesus said that he did not come into this world to be served, but to serve (Mt 20:28). This is what it means to be a minister. To follow Jesus' example into the most humble of jobs and tasks. We should never feel like a job is beneath us to do. This is a clear sign that an adjustment is necessary.

The apostle Paul in 1 Corinthians 12 said that we all have been given spiritual gifts and that these gifts are to be used to help the body and serve the world. So, the two-fold question that each Christian should ask is, "What is my gift?" and "What am I supposed to be doing with it?"

Each of these gifts are different, serving different purposes and were spread out among all the members of the church because they all have one central purpose—to aid in ministering to other believers and to the world around us. The church and her members must not be afraid to discover and exercise the gifts God has given to the church. There should be care and wisdom when we exercise the gifts within the ministries of the church, but to fail to exercise these gifts would be like turning off the power to our homes and then complaining that none of the appliances work. If we are going to see the ministries of the church flourish, we must make use of everything God has made available to us.

If we do not know what gift we have it can be difficult to use for ministry, talk to a pastor and seek their counsel and wisdom. There are many good spiritual gift inventories that can help us discover what gift we have and how best to use it within our church. When we do not know how or where we fit in to God's plan for ministry we may grow frustrated and become discouraged. Don't wait for that to happen. Seek clarity about what God has for you to do as individuals to minister within God's church.

GROWTH POINT

In what ways does the idea of ministry frighten you?

What keeps you from getting involved in a ministry of the church?

Learning To Say, "Yes!"

When we think of the word minister we most often think of someone who is a pastor or who, at the very least, works for a church. This is a misconception that should change, if we still hold to it. The word minister as we discussed above actually means "to serve." Somewhere along the line the divide between professional ministers and the "rest of us" was created and it is a distinction that does not really exist in the scripture. It is an idea, however, that has taken root in the collective consciousness of the people of God. This is an artificial separation. It is not taught in the testimony of the Scriptures and has given some within the body of Christ the mistaken belief that they are not also ministers.

The church in our day must return back to what is most important: ministry. Because we all share in the ministry Jesus left for the church to accomplish, we all bear the burden of participating in the ministry of the local expression of the church we belong to. We ought not to dread doing the work of the church. As believers we have a vested interested in what the church is doing in the world.

Many do not serve because they do not know where to serve. Others fail to serve because they do not know how to serve. Still others fear serving because they believe they have nothing to offer. All of these, while common fears and responses to serving, would be focusing on the wrong thing. Our fear should not be the determining factor on whether we serve the Lord through our local church. Allow me a word of encouragement. Just say "Yes!" to God and allow him to take care of the rest. Whether we are ready to accept it or not, our reservations about serving betray a fundamental lack of trust in God's ability to sustain us. Our service is a witness to our confidence in God to lead and provide through the assignment. Make a decision to trust. Make a decision to take some calculated risks with God.

You may be scared (and you very well should be in some cases), and you may feel ill-equipped, but God is faithful. No fear should cloud your view of God's greatness. It is difficult sometimes, to see beyond what is right in front of us but, that is where we need faith and our community. When we take what we are learning and we join our local faith community in serving God, this is a combination for success. In the end we should remember that obedience is the greatest step of faith. To follow through when God has called us to serve those around us is one decision worthy of our fullest effort. Seek opportunities to serve and allow God to demonstrate his faithfulness.

GROWTH POINT

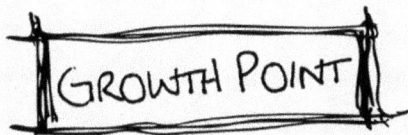

Has the idea of ministry frightened you in the past? If you are not in active ministry right now, what can you do to start?

Ministry is about context, think about some creative ways to serve. What are some needs that you know about in your community that would benefit from your gifts and involvement?

FOUNDATION 3

Service

In the last chapter we looked at ministry as the individual working within and through the context of the corporate body. It is important to make this distinction between ministry and service. Most of us are comfortable with one or the other. By discussing them separately we can better understand how they differ and relate to each other. In this chapter we will explore how we, as individual believers, should make serving others a natural expression of our own faith journey.

Prove It!

One of the more difficult ideas that Jesus proposed to his followers was that we're supposed to love our neighbors as we love ourselves (Mk 12:30-31). Some may take this to mean that we cannot or even should not love our neighbors until we love ourselves, but this would be a misunderstanding of the text. The idea is that we should give to others the kind of love we desire to receive for ourselves. What we are unwilling to give, we should not expect to receive in kind.

One of the most fundamental principles of the kingdom of God is that of sowing and reaping. We must sow first, and then the harvest comes. We give from ourselves, not from some reservoir we have, but out of God's abundant mercy. We do not have the spiritual fortitude to love our neighbors or our enemies. And, we cannot not fabricate it either. Only God can transform our hearts and instill a new nature within us capable of loving like God loves us. We all must depend upon God to fill us with the affections we need for those we encounter in life.

Caring for our neighbor is not something that can be ignored or overlooked as unimportant. Of all the admonitions that Jesus made, he said the love of God and the love of neighbor are the most important. These two are so important and so closely connected they are known singularly as "The Greatest Commandment." Jesus went so far as to say that upon these two commandments hang, hinge, stand "all of the law and the prophets" (Mt 22:34-40, NKJV). Everything we believe and hold to be true can be summarized with these two statements. If we were to take time to properly consider the significance of this is we would be confronted with the unyielding realization that we do not always practice the kind of love Jesus commands. We would see how often we fall to meet the expectation of Christian living in a consistent way.

Another example may help change this idea of loving others even further. There are many religions in the world. And, each of these religions has their own unique characteristics. They may even share some similarities—at least on the surface. However, one of the more striking differences between Christianity and all the other religions of the world is the amazing simplification of essential requirements expected for the devout. What this means is that while other religions in the world want to add more and more regulations to adhere to and fulfill, God says, "Here, just try these two and see how you do."

In Christianity there is an inexplicable shrinking of the requirements demanded of those who practice the faith of Jesus. What I find so striking is the difficulty we all face in fulfilling these two propositions in our lives. A quote attributed to G. K. Chesterton, the great Christian philosopher and writer of the early twentieth century, said, "The Christian ideal has not been tried and found wanting. It has been found difficult, and left untried." This is the reality of our journey. We think that we have tried loving our neighbors. The truth is we looked at our neighbors and decided to relocate, looking for easier neighbors to love.

As we go through this process of growing in faith we come to a very sharp and unyielding challenge. What are we, as individual believers, **DOING** with our faith? James, the brother of Jesus, wrote that faith without works is dead. We say we have faith! Well, James would respond by saying to us, "Show me your faith without your works, and I will show you my faith by my works" (Jas 1:18, NKJV). If nothing has happened since we have confessed our sin, professed faith in Jesus, and have been baptized into the family of God, there should be some cause for concern.

Our faith was not meant solely for ourselves, but for those around us as well. That's why God gave it to us. We have to prove our faith. Better yet, we have to validate the presence of our faith. We do not do this for God's benefit, but to ourselves and to the world. Every action we do because of our love of God and neighbor is a witness to our ongoing transformation. How different are we today than we were the day we first came to faith in Jesus? Can we tell a difference at all? Can others?

GROWTH POINT

What one act of service could you perform this week to demonstrate your faith to those around you?

What obstacles can you identify that have made it difficult to follow through on what you have learned in church or through the Bible?

Find A Place to Serve

When we serve, those acts of service have a way of healing the one who is doing the work. If you want to experience this healing, then you have to try it out for yourself. This is not something that comes from watching, but from doing. We must put our hands to the plow if we are going to see the fruit of that labor (Lk 9:62). Service is not something that can be done vicariously. We will never be able to count someone else's service as our own. It just doesn't work that way.

We live in a society that tells us that we can have it all—at a very reasonable price of course. The lie inherent in the sales pitch is this: We have begun to desire what we should not desire at all. The price demanded for the satisfactions of this world are far too high. We just may not know it yet. But, God does know and he does understand the cost of sin. And the price that God found reasonable for the redemption of sinners was the blood of His Son, Jesus. What makes us think that we can avoid paying any less a price?

We have to understand what this means for us. If we are going to have all that God intends for our lives, then we must also pay the price that has been set, and that price is our service. Full commitment is not easy. As a matter of fact, it's not supposed to be.

Paul's description of our service is both far reaching and insightful. He tells the Romans, "I beseech you therefore, brethren, by the mercies of God, that you present your bodies a living sacrifice, holy, acceptable to God, which is your **reasonable service**" (Rom 12:1, NKJV, emphasis added). It truly can be shocking to read a passage like this—one that I have read hundreds of times—and miss this kernel of truth. It is reasonable to give myself to God totally. Said in the opposite, it is not **unreasonable** for us to give our whole lives to God. Let that sink in. Paul is telling us that what God expects is not unreasonable! We must learn to acknowledge this whenever we are tempted to say that "God would not ask me to..." followed by something we do not want to do.

To serve is to return to where God intended for us to be from the beginning. He commanded Adam to go and tend to the garden. Adam was not created to just recline on the soft grass and eat grapes and do nothing. Adam had a job and it was to see after the creation of God. The older I get the more I realize that it is in doing the simple things God has commanded that I find the most joy. The greater the sacrifice in our acts of service the higher the potential for deep and abiding joy. As we pour our lives out for others the more room we give to God to fill us with his immeasurable grace and empowering love.

```
╔══════════════════════════════╗
║       GROWTH POINT           ║
╚══════════════════════════════╝
```

Do you agree with Paul that our service is "reasonable"? Why or why not?

What Are You Doing?

If there is anything at all that is hard about being a Christian it is this: we have to do something. Inactivity and laziness are not the marks of Christian faithfulness. To sit back and kick our feet up simply will not do. I believe God demands that we become, not just active but proactive. We will not be satisfied if we are not serving God and others. It is unacceptable to do nothing. As a matter of fact, to do nothing may verge on sin.

Let's consider an important question here: When we look at our lives, do we think that God is pleased? This is not a question meant to elicit guilt, even though we may feel it. If we cannot answer this question honestly and in a way that leaves a sense of peace in our hearts, then something has to change, something is going to have to give. I can assure you of this, God will not be the one doing the moving.

The reality of our faith journey is this, we are to live a life marked by action. We are not to be idle or complacent. God has called and is calling us to a deeper commitment to the privilege of serving those around us. The more we engage in acts and opportunities of service the better we embody the example of Jesus. For many of us, we have not been encouraged to serve sacrificially. We need more examples of Christ-like service, not less. When we do not know what that looks like we have a tendency to stay still.

Whenever I feel this tendency toward inactivity I remember a verse from the Psalms. It is a simple idea that has helped get me moving again. King David said it like this: "The steps of a good man are ordered by the LORD: and he delighteth in his way" (KJV). While there are two possible understandings of this passage, the context would lend itself to the view that the "good man" is the one who delights in the way the LORD has ordered. If we desire for our steps to be according to God's will then we must move in faith and trust where God is leading.

A practical implication of this verse when I read or recall it is if I am not moving there are no steps to order. As I am walking along life's road God is directing me and guiding me, if I allow and invite his direction. Also, do you see what else is happening? David says that because of this process of my moving and God's ordering, I am finding delight (i.e., joy and satisfaction) in the process. What this means is for us is that when we trust the Lord to direct our way the chances of greater joy are multiplied.

It is true that no one—other than God—may be able to judge the implementation of the measure of faith that God has provided for us to use. But, the world outside the church will. The world can see and consider the effect (or lack thereof) that our professed faith has had in our lives and in the lives of those within our circle of influence. Let's begin to ask God to increase our desire to serve, to share the love we have experienced with those around us. We have to ask ourselves, "What does the world see?" The better question may be, "what should they see when they see us coming their way?"

GROWTH POINT

List any possible reasons for not serving more regularly. Beside each reason write what you can do to change this reason into an opportunity.

FOUNDATION 4

Participation (Time)

What Do You Value?

I have heard people say that by looking at someone's checkbook it will provide some insight into how their money is being spent and thereby a picture of what they value. So, if I were to look at the register of your life what would it say you are spending your *life* on? The simple truth is that what we give to most is what, in the end, we value most. This is not a comment of criticism, but a reality we could all agree with, at least generally.

When I look at what I do with these few precious moments I have been given in and on this world, I have to ask, "What good is coming of my being here on this earth?" When the time comes for all of us, and it will, when we will breathe our last breath, will what we remember be memories of a life filled with years or years filled with life? We must never lose sight of the gift of our time here on this earth. The scripture tells us that tomorrow is not promised to any of us (cf. Lk 12:13-21; Pro 27:1). I don't say this to scare you into being more cautious. Rather, it is a call to live more intentionally today.

Being a Christian means that we have made a choice. Whether we understood it completely or not the choice was made. It was a choice to live by a certain code of morals, ethics, and values. The choice was to change the way we were living our lives because we had met someone who showed us there was a better way to live. A vote of confidence in Jesus is a vote of no confidence in ourselves—that we cannot find the best way, let alone live that way on our own, in our own strength. I think it is an injustice to new Christians not to explain this to them. If a plant is not growing or bearing fruit the assumption, often times, is that there must be something wrong. It may even be dead. How are we doing? Are we bearing fruit or are we just giving an appearance of life?

What we value will cause us to reorient our lives around it. We all should carefully consider what we value because if it is not worth the price of our lives we may have made something into an idol that is not worthy of our worship. Have you ever considered the giving of your time and effort to something as worship? How about this, have you ever heard someone say that they do something religiously? What we give our time to reveals our devotion and commitment to it.

The last word that John left in his first letter is both interesting and provocative and sheds some light on what we are talking about. John provides encouragement for believers to love one another as Jesus loves us; to protect ourselves from the temptations of the world; to be watchful of those who would distract us from God. The letter is filled with all manner of insights and yet it ends, rather abruptly, with the warning to "keep yourselves from idols" (1 Jn 5:21, ESV).

Usually the last thing someone says the one thing you remember best, and this phrase is no exception. I have always found this to be an unusual way of ending the letter. However, when you consider that the greatest enemy to our relationship with God is another "god," you begin to understand the warning. When our attention is drawn to something, else other than God, we are drifting into the sin called idolatry. Idolatry is the placing of our trust in anything other than God for the purpose of getting our identity from it. John reminds us to be careful of this temptation.

GROWTH POINT

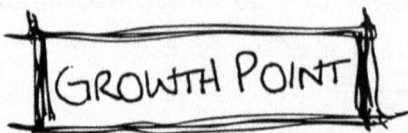

Is there something in your life that is distracting you from focusing on God and his purposes in your life?

Growth Does Not Happen in a Vacuum

If we have a genuine desire for the choice we made for Christ to be reflected in our lives, we have to make time for learning, practicing, and doing what we claim is important. A baby must be encouraged to walk, even though parents know they will fall. Parents do this because there will come a time when the parent will not be around to catch them. And when that time comes will the child be ready? In a similar way, all of us are children of God. Some of us are still babes, still trying to establish our footing in this new faith. Others are now able to put the lessons learned into practice. And still others are now the teachers bringing their maturity full circle and helping the babies learn to walk on their own.

The church is the place God has designated for us to gather together to learn and grow and practice what God is teaching through his Word. The church is what Jesus said he would build. And it is the only thing God will use to accomplish his purposes in the world. When we forget this we hinder our own development but, we also hamper the spiritual development of others in our local fellowships.

There was a time that I would grumble and complain about all that was wrong with the church. I no longer do that. There are several reasons why, but I will give two here. First, the church is Christ's body. When I complain about the church or have a negative view of the church I am complaining against Jesus. We should take greater care of what we say about the church. The world will take their cues from us and what we say about Christ's body.

Second, the church is Jesus' bride. I would never tolerate anyone talking negatively of my wife. As a matter of fact, I would like to think that I would defend the wife of a friend. In both of these cases, in order to defend my wife or the wife of friend I have to maintain a positive view and acknowledge the inherent value of the person I am defending. Christian's should not bad mouth the church and they should not participate (whether passively or actively) in tearing down the one institution Jesus said he would build!

This discussion of the church is important. The first reason we discussed above reminds us that Jesus values the church. The second reason is equally worthy of considering. We have to consider if we value the church enough to stay connected it. Our spiritual health and growth is joined to the health of the church. When we become disconnected from the body of Jesus we jeopardize and stunt our development. The church is God's plan. We should work to better understand the plan rather than thinking we can come up with a better one.

We should try and determine what value the church has to us. When we do we are in a better position to achieve clarity regarding our connection to it. Some have mockingly asked, "Are we supposed to go to church every day?" This question reveals an assumption that often times goes unnoticed and unchallenged. The church is not a building. The church is a gathering of people. This means that the first step we should take is to change how we ask the question. A better question would be, "How often should I gather **WITH** the church?" When we ask the question this way we change the focus and make the first foundation—Fellowship—a priority in our decision making. In light of this new understanding it would be to the benefit of every believer to meet with the church as often as possible. Our hearts should stay close to those who are striving to stay close to God.

Jesus told his disciples that whenever two or three are gathered together in his name, he would be present. This is a remarkable promise. It also reveals that the church can be expressed with as few as two or three people. If I gather with another brother or sister in Christ and we do so with the purpose of honoring Christ, there, at that moment, the church is gathered.

We also have to understand that our growth as a follower of Christ depends on our connection to God. I have had people say to me, "I don't need to go to church to be a Christian." This statement, on its face, is true. However, I now have a response to this statement. "You may not need to go to church to be a Christian, but you need to go to church to learn how to be a good one." This is one of many ways of capturing the essential reality that we all need to be connected to the body Jesus created. The church exists to reconcile lost sinners with a holy God and restore these redeemed individuals to fellowship with God's people. We are not saved to then live in isolation.

No matter how I feel about the people who

make up the church, it is the place where I discover my new identity in Christ and practice the faith I now confess to believe. Pastor Luis Scott often says, "It is an absolute miracle that the church has survived for 2,000 years considering the kind of people who make it up." He is correct. The church is filled with self-professed sinners. This is why we all should demonstrate greater charity in the church than in any other place in the world. When it is not present we should ask ourselves, "What can I do to make it better?" Our response should not be to run away, complaining about "those" sinners in there. We are all to become part of the solution.

The bottom line is this. We should desire to be with the church. Our journey of faith can only be sustained, nurtured, and challenged to grow when we get connected and stay connected to God's people. Our development as Christians does not occur in a vacuum. We grow in community. Therefore, find one and get plugged in to what God is doing there.

Going to meet with the church or not going should not feel like a guilt trip. If it does, then there are some issues that must be addressed. I am not always able to go meet with my home church, but that does not mean that I will not go somewhere else if I can and gather with my extended family of faith. Regardless of how we feel, go should go and meet with the church because we desire to be around God and God makes himself present when his people gather together (Psalm 22:3).

GROWTH POINT

Have you understood the church as a building or a gathering of people? How has this affected your attendance?

Take Part in the Process

Participation is a growing pain and a vital foundation because it demands that we reevaluate the time that we spend away from the priorities of God's agenda for his Kingdom. I will grant that life as a

Christian will seem overwhelming at times but, there is no substitute for time spent with God and with brothers and sisters in Christ. Being born-again means that we have a new family with new values and a new way of looking at the world. We have to learn how to reprioritize our activities in ways that agree with what is important to God, and this will take some effort. What we have to watch out for is making the effort an excuse for not making any movement toward change.

Begin to take an active part in the process of your spiritual growth and development. This means getting connected and staying connected to the local fellowship to which God has called you. In a lot of ways, faith is a muscle that must be exercised and the gym for proper training is the church. Take part in the process because this is a marathon, not a sprint. I will offer this challenge as it relates to your participation in and with the church: Go to your pastor and ask, "What needs to be done that no one else wants to do?" Then, go and do it with joy. Remember you asked for it, so don't complain!

If we make our participation with the church a priority in our lives there is going to be a lasting, positive effect in both our lives and in the lives of those around you. As we have seen, the church is God's plan for accomplishing his will. Our commitment to the church is part of that plan as well.

GROWTH POINT

What is one step you can take today to become more active in the process of your spiritual growth and development?

FOUNDATION 5

Discipleship

Being Stretched

One of the most challenging obstacles that we must face in life is ourselves. For the most part there is no greater barrier to spiritual growth than our own preconceived and long standing beliefs—or miss-beliefs. It can be difficult to get rid of ideas and thoughts that have guided us because we believed they were good and right. This is more the case for adults than for children because when a child comes to Christ they have not experienced much of life. The time needed to form opinions and solidify convictions is still in a state of flux.

A child comes in innocence. Through the love and structure of a church and family they learn the faith, being formed spiritually and physically. The spiritual and physical aspects of a child's life have a chance of growing in tandem (assuming the family is intentional about discipling the child as they mature.) Because what they learn is gradual, the need to replace or undo other ideas and feelings and thoughts from outside sources is reduced.

A child asks this question, "Is what I have been taught the truth?" This will be the struggle of the child raised in the church. Helping a child move from what they have been taught to believe, to the practice of faith is the journey they will travel. That is why every young believer should be surrounded by mentors and godly examples so these people can help the child process and internalize the faith. Every person who grows up in a Christian home will all be faced with the choice of whether they want to live according to what they were taught. The hazards here are innumerable because if the parents were not fully committed to Jesus then it is hard to know how a child will interpret the lessons they received while at home.

An adult who comes to faith in Jesus, on the other hand, asks a different question. An adult's question is, "Why should I change what I already believe and hold to be true to what the Gospel promotes?" This question highlights the difference between a child coming to faith and an adult. This struggles is what causes the stretching in most people's lives. If we came to faith in Christ as adults we have already lived for some time guided by certain assumptions, presuppositions, and principles. Now that these have been challenged, the process of conforming our lives to more accurately reflect the image of Jesus will begin in earnest.

For the child it is a struggle to hold on to what he or she has been taught. For the adult it is the process of replacing already held beliefs for Christian ones. And it is through the process of discipleship provided by the church that the stretching and change occurs. It is through the struggle of finding the truth and learning to exercise faith for ourselves that we become more like Jesus. In the church we should avoid any standardized timetables as it relates to anyone's spiritual development. We all grow at our own pace.

At the most basic level, discipleship is the process of becoming like Jesus. It is the way Jesus himself formed the original apostles. It is the way that the church helps men and women become people who believe, live, and do the things that Jesus taught. To be a Christian disciple is to become as Christ to the world. We are to become images, pure and perfect reflections, of Jesus, so that when the world looks at us they think of and see Jesus. The word "Christian" literally means "a little Christ." That is what the church is designed to reproduce in each of its members. In every person the image of Jesus should be present.

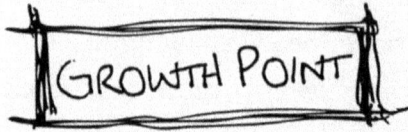

What scares you the most about the idea of become more like Jesus? Why?

From Milk to Meat

At the beginning of the Apostle Paul's first letter to the Corinthian church he reveals his amazement that some in the church were still behaving carnally (1 Cor 3:1). What that means is they were still trying to live a Christian life according to the rules and principles of the world. The temptation and tendency toward carnality is one of the primary reasons for entering into a discipleship journey. The discipleship process helps every Christian identify and work to minimize this tendency in our lives. We do not always know how much of the world's way of thinking has infiltrated our own. We do not always know when the principles and thinking of the world will surface in our lives. Therefore, it becomes vitally important to receive and apply the lessons and instruction we receive through our church's discipleship process.

Paul's description in 1 Corinthians is that there were some who were still drinking spiritual milk and had not moved on to meat, which represented maturity and advancement in the ways of God. In short, Paul was saying that there were members in the church who had shown no signs of maturity at all. As difficult as it may be to believe, we should not assume that anyone is mature—including ourselves—just because we have been born again for a long time. Spiritual maturity is not something we control. God is the one who grows us up, and that when we submit ourselves to the discipleship process and spiritual oversight of our local church.

What appears to have been happening in the church in Corinth was that there were a significant number of people whose growth and development had been stunted. The reason? Paul tells us that the Christians in Corinth were not living out the teaching they had been given. If the body grows through physical food, how does the spirit grow? The spirit grows through spiritual food. The practices of scripture reading, prayer, worship, fellowship and service are ways that we learn, live, and do the Christian faith. The seven FOUNDATIONS we are discussing in this book are the basic practices every believer should strive to cultivate.

The difference between milk and meat is this, milk is the easy to do stuff. It is the beginning of the journey. Milk is the "talk" of faith, but as we mature we move to the meat, the "walk" of faith. The practice of faith is actually doing what we say we believe. This is where claiming to be a Christian becomes more difficult. We begin to move and act in ways that embody the talk of faith. From suckling on a mother's breast to eating T-bone steaks is a journey of years in the physical sense. Spiritual development can be an equally difficult and time consuming process.

Most of us should not expect to become spiritually mature overnight. We should not be discouraged by this either. As a matter of fact, this can be encouraging when we find ourselves struggling with letting go of former habits. We are not alone in this journey. There are others who have been walking this walk of faith for many years. Seek their counsel and wisdom. Pride is the greatest enemy of maturity.

What tends to happen at the beginning of our journey, and even further down the road, is thinking that worldly wisdom can be converted to spiritual wisdom. This will never work like we would like because the wisdom of this world is not like the wisdom we receive from above (1 Cor 3:19; c.f., 1 Cor 1:20-21, 25-31). The wisdom we receive from God is of a different kind and is intended for a different purpose—to make us more like Jesus. Worldly wisdom is not designed for this purpose. We should ask our Heavenly Father to help us grow in the wisdom he offers to provide (Jas 1:5).

GROWTH POINT

Do you believe that your talk of faith and your walk of faith are consistent? Why or Why not?

It Begins With a Step

There are few things worse in life than finding out we are not as knowledgeable on a given subject as we thought. This causes us to become embarrassed by our own ignorance. It is difficult to hide from ourselves when we are confronted with our deficiencies. The irony is that this is true of an adult but not a baby. A baby does not have its pride hurt when she is hungry and asks for food by crying. An infant has no concept of pride, it merely reacts to the natural yearnings her little body is indicating.

The older we get the more we have to fight against pride in our lives. Our spiritual hunger should cause us to cry out for spiritual food without shame or reservation. It should be natural. What is unnatural is going hungry and stifling our own spiritual growth. Under different circumstances this would be considered foolish thinking. It is truly amazing how we allow ourselves to become discouraged and sidetracked on our spiritual journey because of prideful embarrassment. Responding to our spiritual hunger by denying its presence can have long-lasting, harmful effects.

The problem may now be that we no longer recognize our hunger for what it is. Spiritual malnourishment is not easy to diagnose. But, its effects are easier to identify. Fear, anger, spiritual apathy, and the lack of desire to practice and participate in the foundations are a clear indication that we have gotten off track.

The first realization in growing up is admitting that we do not fundamentally know everything we need in order to survive. As we grow we come to a better understanding of some of our own needs. But, if we do not have someone supervising our growth we risk malnutrition. The longer we avoid taking this first step—of admitting we need help to grow spiritually— the longer it will take for our maturity to get on track.

As we get connected and stay connected to the local church we develop the tools and acquire the wisdom we need to understand our own maturing process. In a similar process to that mirrors our physical development, we have to be taught many things with regard to our spiritual growth. When we assume we understand what we need to grow spiritually we make mistakes. Mistakes we could have avoided and learned from those around us.

Discipleship is the process that gives us insight into what we need so that we can begin to ask for more of what God has for us. The process can feel overwhelming at first because we don't know where to start. I think James offered us a good starting point when he said, "You do not have because you do not ask" (Jas 4: 2, NKJV). As growing people, we must be honest with ourselves if we want a chance to grow in faith but, we must also be patient. Take the first step. Discipleship will take time and will be worth the effort.

GROWTH POINT

Where do you think you are on the maturity scale? What is a next step you can take to continue to grow? If you are not sure, ask a pastor in your church or a friend you consider to be "ahead" of you on the journey of faith.

FOUNDATION 6

Evangelism

Give What Has Been Given

If there is one characteristic that encapsulates the essence of Christianity it would have to be selflessness. Jesus was the ultimate example of this when he allowed himself to be crucified for sinners. Another word we can use is humility. Rick Warren wrote in *The Purpose Driven Life* that humility is not thinking less of yourself, it is thinking of yourself less.

While this is a helpful reminder it would only be part of the picture. The idea we must grapple with in this chapter is that there has to be a shift in how we understand what it means to be humble. Too often, there are calls for others to be more humble and yet the ones calling for greater humility are themselves doing so from a position of pride. Humility is a posture of the heart, not a behavior. Until we understand this we will never comprehend what we are supposed to be doing as it relates to our Christian walk.

We start this chapter discussing humility because it is, in my estimation, the bedrock of evangelism. We do not share the Gospel of Jesus because we are better than anyone else. We share the Gospel precisely because we are not better than anyone else. It has been famously said that the ground is level at the foot of the cross. This means that every person is a sinner with the same degree of culpability before God. Any evangelistic efforts we engage in ought to proceed from a heart humbled by the knowledge of how God has forgiven us our own sin.

One of the aspects of the Christian life that often gets relegated to the "I'll do it if I get a chance" heap is evangelism. This should not be. This is due to the fact that one of the key realities of being the people that God redeemed is that we must be willing to share the Good News of Jesus to all who within our sphere of influence. If we have been forgiven so much; if we have been blessed so much; if we have been transformed so much by the Gospel, why do we find ourselves hesitating to share the message that has done so much for us?

The sharing of the Gospel message within our circles of influence begins with an assessment of our own heart. More specifically, we have to evaluate the reasons (or excuses) we use for not doing it at all. If we are ever going to engage in evangelistic endeavors we must evaluate our own motivations. Until we do, we will stay on the sidelines, rather than joining the church is spreading the message of Good News in and to the world.

There is a phrase that has been stuck in my mind from the time I first heard it. It is borrowed, but it says, "God will not send a blessing to you, if He knows He can't get it through you." At first I was not sure how true it was. However, as I have considered what it implies about us as the recipients of God's blessing I began to understand it better. God's hand and activity in our lives is not about us, and it surely is not only for us. God does not need us to accomplish his purposes, but when we surrender our lives in repentance and obedience we have put ourselves at God's disposal. My father has often said that he wants to be so available to God that God has no choice but to use him. Is that our desire as well? Or do we just stand in line and hope not to be picked because we'd like to ride the bench?

Early in the book (Chapter 3) we discussed that the Christian faith functions according the principle of sowing and reaping. This can also be described as the principle of return. What this means is that no one comes to faith in isolation. The growth and spread of faith requires a body of believers to pass it on to others. If we had never seen a church, a Christian, or a Bible we never would have known about Jesus. We may have thought about God but that would be the extent of it. The Apostle Paul said that the world, the creation, testifies of God (Rom 1:20). However, this general revelation is not enough if what we need is to have a reconciled relationship with God.

In order to enter into this necessary relationship we have to be exposed to the special revelation of the Gospel. In his letter to the Colossian church Paul shares what has happened in the world because of Jesus' ministry. Paul told them of "the mystery hidden for ages and generations but now revealed to his saints" (Col 1:26, ESV). God was waiting for an appointed time to reveal what he had planned in eternity to do through Jesus' life, death, and resurrection (Gal 4:4-5). This plan cannot be known through human reason or investigation. This plan must be revealed by the one who conceived of the strategy and guarded the secret.

The amazing paradox of this hidden message that has now been revealed is that the task of spreading the Gospel—this eternal, life given news—has been given and entrusted to the Church of Jesus (2 Cor 5:19c). We have been called to be ambassadors to the world. So, what is God doing through us as his ambassadors? God is "making his appeal through us," therefore, "we implore you on behalf of Christ, be reconciled to God" (2 Cor 5:20, ESV). We, as members of the body of Christ, have become the emissaries of the kingdom of God to the world.

What does all this mean for us? It means that if there has been any benefit or change in our lives because of the Gospel of Jesus, then we are charged with a great responsibility. We have been enlisted to join in the task taking the Gospel to the ends of the earth. Anything less could be considered a dereliction of our duties to God.

We have been commissioned to give what has been given to us to as many people as we can find. Our responsibility in evangelism is to share the Gospel, to pass it along to those who come across our journey. We cannot control what happens after we share it. We are only asked to engage in the process. We plant and we water, but only God can cause that seed to grow and give a harvest.

In the Gospel we find all that God has promised to those who believe. We see the fulfillment of every good thing God has for us. When we believe the Gospel we are given access to God himself. This is a miracle. As sinners we could never approach the throne of God. But, as adopted children, we have been given the same privileges as Jesus, the true and natural-born son.

The Bible plainly declares that the power of the

Gospel is bringing about salvation of lost souls. It is this salvation that brings about eternal joy to the broken spirit and the wounded heart of humanity. We can drink deeply from rivers of joy when we give to others what we have received in Jesus by faith.

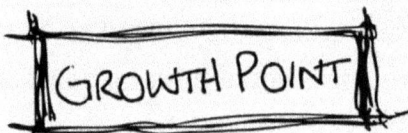

GROWTH POINT

Do you have a desire to share with others the Gospel of Jesus? Why or why not?

Many Ways to Share

Far too many Christians have been turned off to evangelism because they think it means to spread the message of Jesus because of some extreme examples labeled as evangelism. For many the word evangelism conjures up images of getting on a soapbox on a street corner or handing out tracts door-to-door or being able to quote scripture from memory to someone who is not a Christian. Evangelism is more than what you know or do not know about the church, the Bible or the doctrines of Scripture. I believe evangelism can be summarized by answering one question: What has Jesus done for us that is worth sharing with someone else? If we can think of one thing (and we should be able to) that Jesus has done for us, then that is what we should share. It does not have to be more complicated than that.

I do not believe "Bible thumping" is what Jesus had in mind when he sent his disciples out. Can we take a warm meal to a family who is mourning the death of a loved one? This is evangelism. Can we tell someone of a prayer that God has answered? Can we show grace where once there would have been anger or bitterness or resentment? This is what evangelism looks like.

Some may feel comfortable with a more confrontational method. There are people who need this kind of straightforward talk but, there are others who could use a gentle hug of comfort or a kind word of hope. The Gospel is supposed to be a balm, a medicine that we apply to the pains and hurts of someone's life and spirit. If this is true, then it should not feel like alcohol on an open wound.

As growing believers we should discover a variety ways of sharing the message of Jesus. We need to know what we are comfortable doing. But, we also need to learn a variety of ways of sharing the Gospel so a person actually hears what we are saying. Evangelism is not about a particular method or a program. Evangelism is about exposing more people to the love and grace of God.

GROWTH POINT

What has Jesus done for you? Will you commit to sharing it? (Pray that God would open a door to share what Jesus has done.)

Like A Vitamin

Sharing our faith with someone else is like taking a vitamin. The more and the longer we practice sharing our faith the better we feel and the stronger our faith will become. I share my faith by showing that it is possible to have fun, to have a full and vibrant life and while not compromising my values and convictions.

The image that most people have of the church and Christians has become very negative. There was a time when men and women knew that they needed God in their lives. And, they knew that they could make that connection in the church. There are so many distractions and diversions today; God has been relegated to an "as needed" remedy.

There are many people who feel that with a good job and good income they can get everything they need. We are living in a time where people can chose their own way of doing things. There is no longer any thought given to the truth because truth is now subjective and relative. The form of evangelism must change to meet the growing challenges our contemporary context presents. But the substance must be guarded and cannot change.

We have to find ways of engaging in spiritual conversations. If our faith is important to us, then talking about it should become as "normal" a subject of conversation as breathing. Remember, you are not trying to change anyone. The goal is to develop friendships and relationships with people who don't know Jesus, so that we might have an opportunity to share the Gospel so they can believe and exercise faith for themselves. We should strive to find opportunities every day to speak of what God has been doing in our lives. And that is evangelism at its core.

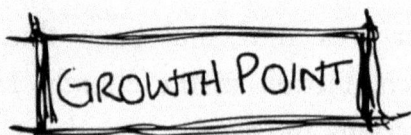

GROWTH POINT

Make a commitment to intentionally talk about Jesus to someone this week. Pick something that you read in Bible recently; a topic covered in a sermon or Bible study. Think about what you want to say and write it down here. Practice with your spouse or a friend.

FOUNDATION 7

Changing Circles

Difficult Choices

What happens when we make decisions that force us to change the way we think or how we live our lives? Things start to get tough, that's what happens. It can be difficult to change the way we do things. How much more difficult can those changes be for our families and friends who are not believers or who do not understand our growing relationship with God? If we have Christian family and friends we should count ourselves blessed. However, there are many who make a decision for Christ and find themselves cast out and pushed away by those they love.

It is not easy to choose Christ anymore. The path becomes more difficult and it no longer appears smooth. We begin to see how the journey can cost us in areas and in ways we could not even begin to imagine. This is the primary reason this foundation and growing pain appears last. The first six are vitally important for new believers who will have to change the circles they are a part of.

To live the Christian life, to live it as it is meant to be lived, will require difficult choices. And these choices are difficult because some of these choices may require us to change the circle, or circles, of influence in our lives. A circle of influence consists of those individuals that we listen to and trust. The reason that a change may be needed is not because a person is "bad," but because our values have changed. Our worldview and perspective have shifted and we no longer align ourselves with the crowd we were a part of. The reasons and motivations of our lives have changed and if someone does not share these convictions with us then something will give way. Something must give. It inevitably does, so we should not be surprised when it happens. The question then is what do we do if a believer does not have a place to go? They will probably return to what they used to know. They will fill into previous patterns or even embrace new, harmful ones.

Having said this, I want to make it clear that changing circles does not mean that you must let go of the relationships forever or even at all. What changing circles means is that the ear that at one time was ready to hear from any and every source must now filter words and intentions that do not agree with the Word of God. We no longer allow just anyone access to the way that we think or feel. We become more discerning of who we listen to and what we allow in our lives.

We all have to learn how to sift out those things in our lives that are inconsistent with our faith. The hardest aspect of changing circles is that it is a conscious choice we have to make. God is not going to force us to choose him. We must make that choice within our own hearts for ourselves.

GROWTH POINT

When you consider your decision to follow Jesus, did you consider that you would have to be more careful with who you listened to?

What influences will you have to consider changing and letting go of?

Stay Connected

Our change in circles begins with hearing the truth of the Gospel. The Gospel is what forces us to reconsider who and what we allow to influence us in our lives. After we have heard the message of good news and have been received by Christ into the family of God, we begin to experience the conviction of the Holy Spirit who moves us to make a profession of faith. We confess and repent of our sins, accept Jesus as Lord and are baptized, seeking to join a local body of believers. As we grow in faith we are encouraged to go and share what has happened. We are awakened to the wonderful transformation that has happened. But, what do we do when we do not get the reaction that we wanted or even expected from those closest to us?

We can be left wondering whether or not the decision we made was the correct one because the ones who have helped and counseled us throughout our lives do not seem to agree with what we have decided. Even for those of us within the church, what God has done or is doing is not always well received by friends and family. What we are not told from the beginning of our life of faith is that no two people will experience the same set of circumstances or learning experiences on our journey with God. My journey is unique because my relationship to God is just as distinct. We must never forget this.

One of the primary dangers every new and young Christian faces will be the temptation to go back to the "old life." This is both not surprising, but it should also be something to look out for. Connecting to a church that will provide direction and protection in the early stages of growth is vital. None of us can stay disconnected for long and expect to flourish.

I remember hearing about a pastor that went to visit a member of the church who had stopped attending. He knocked on the door and was received by the man. The pastor walked in silently and both men sat in the chairs that were facing the fire gently dancing in the fireplace. After a few minutes of silence the man grabbed a poker and pulled one of the coals from the fire. A few minutes later the coal had stopped glowing the bright red it once emitted when in the fireplace. The pastor, without saying a word, then proceeded to grab the same poker and gently pushed the now cold peace of coal back into the fire. After yet another few minutes the lump had reignited and was again a bright red. The man looked at the pastor and said, "Thank you for the fiery sermon. I will be at church on Sunday."

What is the lesson? Our connection to the body of Christ is what keeps the fires of faith going in our lives. The greater the distance from God's people, the farther we are from experiencing the influence of God upon our lives.

We all reach a crossroads on this journey of faith. There will be more than one, but there is one that will serve as a defining moment for how we will deal with all the others. This point of decision is where the difficult decision to be obedient to God is made. What this fundamentally means is this: We have to ask ourselves whose voice will win out?

We have to make the choice because we cannot continue in the old way of doing things. It must be made because we have been changed and have become new creations in and through Christ (2 Cor 5:17). It must be made because if we are going to have any chance of seeing what God intends for us we must be willing to make and live out the decision to obey him. Finally, we have to trust that God will finish what he has started in us (Phil 1:6). This is a promise that God will fulfill.

GROWTH POINT

Think back on your journey with God. Can you identify the moment when you finally made the decision to be obedient to God? What made that moment significant? If not, what is holding you back from making that decision today?

God Wants You to Grow

Ultimately the most important relationship that we nurture in our lives is the one we have with our heavenly Father. Because of this, it is important to surround ourselves with individuals who are also seeking to deepen their relationship with God and who will provide us with the environment, structure, education, and encouragement we need to make our faith a lifelong reality.

There are few things more unfortunate than a person who professes faith with their words but is unable to project a true faith in their lives. It is possible to say we have faith but, that faith is not real to us. It is an illusion rather than a reality. We all should strive to internalize the faith be profess so it produces fruit in our daily walk. If faith is nothing more than a mere theory, an idea of what we wish we had, it will not sustain us. A true and living faith will only come when what we are able to embody what we claim to believe. When we say to ourselves that we will do whatever it takes to live out what we have learned that God desires. This, in the end, is why it becomes so important to change circles.

We are talking about our hearts. Our souls. Our eternal destiny. We are talking about the kind of life we could live and the direction of our lives. We are talking about the lives of our families and the role we play in that. It is time to give ourselves to living the life we have chosen. We made the choice. Now we have to own it.

GROWTH POINT

Take a few minutes and write a pray asking for the help, strength, and wisdom God offers and you need to live out your faith.

CONCLUSION

The Journey Begins

These seven foundations truly are growing pains and growing edges in each of our lives and in the life of the local church we are a part of. As we continue to grow in our understanding of faith, we each have to see that we have been called to be a part of a community of faith. As we become better Christians we are becoming better members of Christ's body.

We should all strive to be obedient to our savior Jesus Christ. The difficult part of living out our faith is the tension we feel in trying to predict how everything is going to end up. We must accept that we may never fully understand what God is up to. As a matter of fact, I do not think we are supposed to. If we try and live our entire lives wondering how each choice we make will impact our future choices we may become paralyzed with insecurities and doubts. But, we cannot live that way. Faith is a dangerous proposition because it challenges us to trust God more than we trust ourselves. Faith makes promises and guarantees that we may find hard to believe but, they can be counted on because of the character of the one who made them. God has never and will never fail to uphold his word.

Now that we know what these foundations are and the role they play in our growth and the health of the church, the journey can begin. I would encourage every reader to pray about their journey of faith journey keeping in mind these seven areas. Ask the following questions as a way of gaging where to focus moving forward:

1. How am I doing in each area?
2. Is there something that I know I need to change, but have been unwilling to act on?
3. Who can I talk to that can help me identify my growing edges?
4. Why do I have such a hard time in the area of _____?

As we go through the process of identifying and growing in each area give thanks to God for never giving up on us. Give thanks for the brothers and sisters in the faith who journey with us. And, most importantly give thanks that we are building our lives on the most solid foundation of all, our Lord and Savior Jesus the Christ.

About the Author

Victor R. Scott currently serves as the *Executive Pastor* for Ministry Development and Discipleship at *Ambassadors of Christ Ministries* in Columbus, Georgia, where he is active in one-on-one discipleship with youth, adults, and pastors using the "Contextualized Reading" method.

He graduated from Georgia Southern University in 2002 with his undergraduate degree. He completed his *Master of Divinity* degree from Luther Rice University and Seminary (2011).

Victor married his high school sweetheart and has two daughters who share the same birthday, four years apart.

www.ingramcontent.com/pod-product-compliance
Lightning Source LLC
Chambersburg PA
CBHW071621040426
42452CB00009B/1425